CHRISTMAS VOCAL DUETS

Intermediate-level Christmas song arrangements for any combination of 2 voices and piano.

ISBN 978-1-70516-829-5

HAL•LEONARD®

Visit Hal Leonard Online at
www.halleonard.com

World headquarters, contact:
Hal Leonard
7777 West Bluemound Road
Milwaukee, WI 53213
Email: info@halleonard.com

In Europe, contact:
Hal Leonard Europe Limited
1 Red Place
London, W1K 6PL
Email: info@halleonardeurope.com

In Australia, contact:
Hal Leonard Australia Pty. Ltd.
4 Lentara Court
Cheltenham, Victoria, 3192 Australia
Email: info@halleonard.com.au

CONTENTS

BELIEVE
from Warner Bros. Pictures' THE POLAR EXPRESS

Words and Music by GLEN BALLARD
and ALAN SILVESTRI

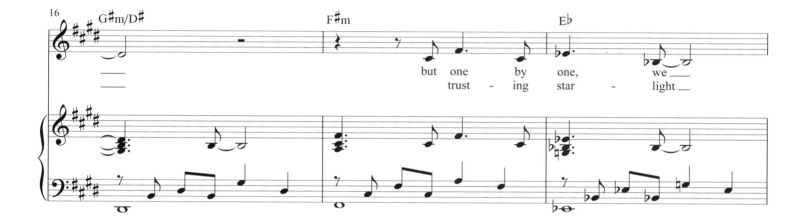

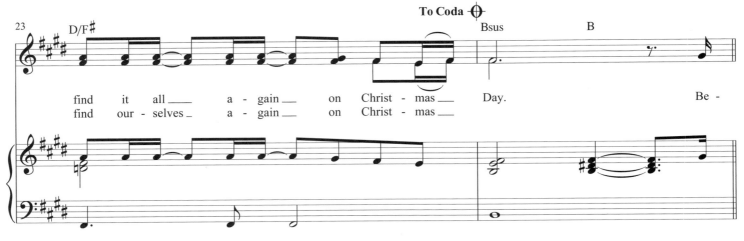

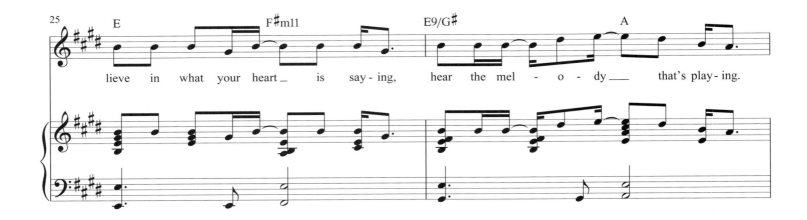

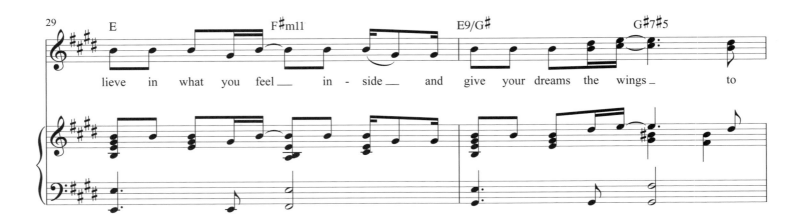

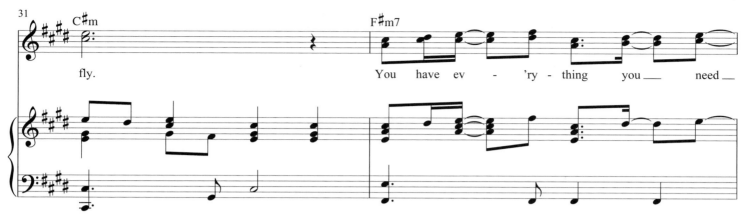

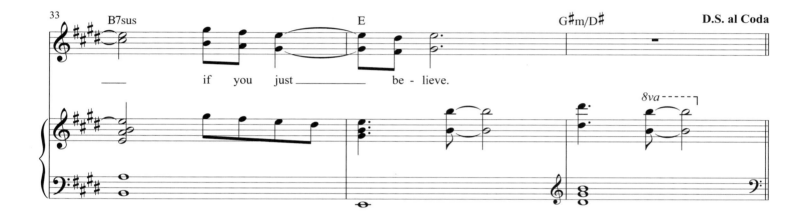

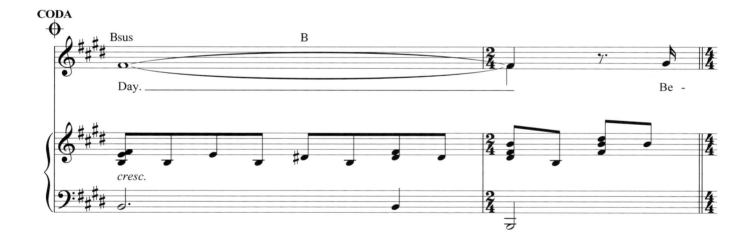

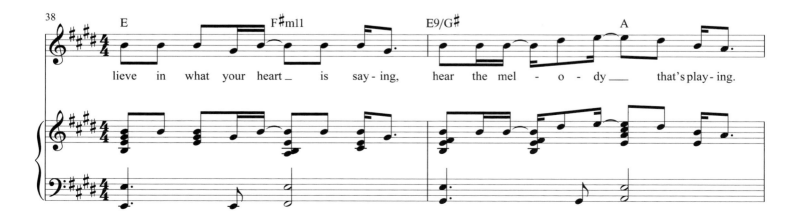

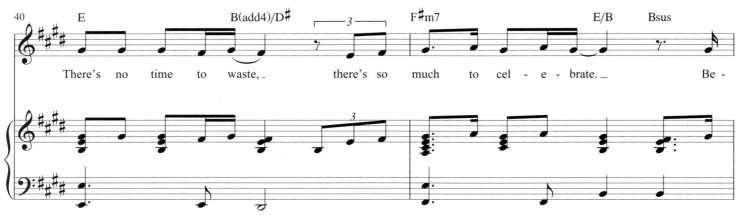

There's no time to waste, _ there's so much to cel - e - brate. _ Be -

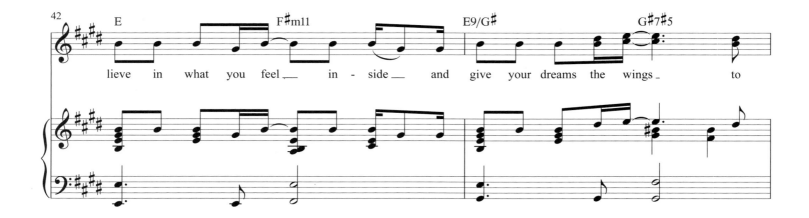

lieve in what you feel _ in - side _ and give your dreams the wings _ to

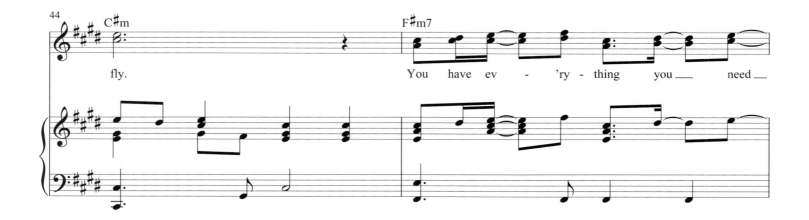

fly. You have ev - 'ry - thing you _ need _

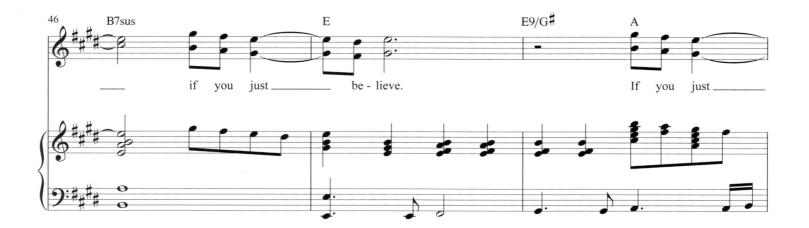

_ if you just _____ be - lieve. If you just ____

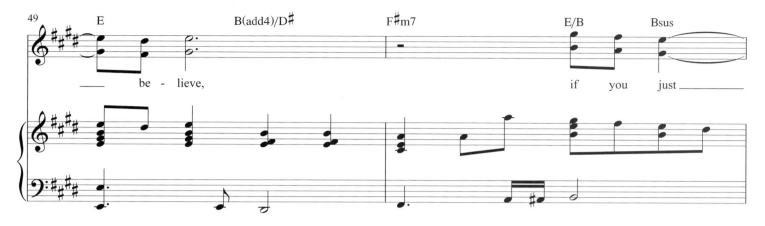

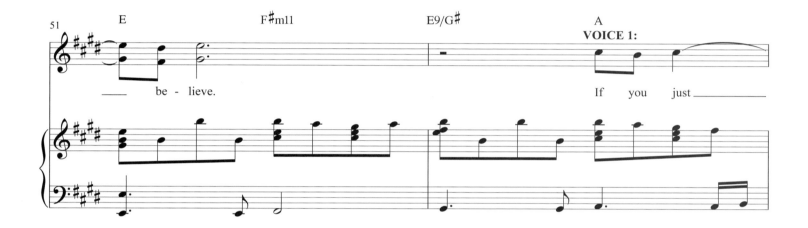

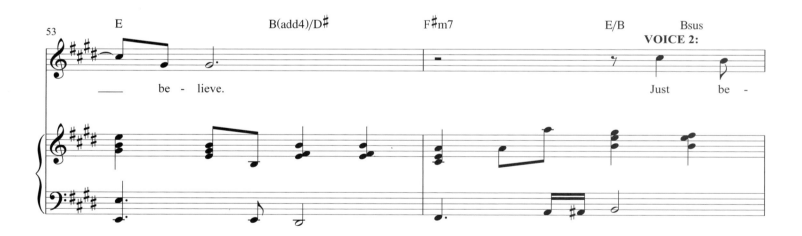

THE CHRISTMAS SONG
(Chestnuts Roasting on an Open Fire)

Music and Lyric by MEL TORMÉ
and ROBERT WELLS

help to make the sea - son bright. Ti - ny tots with their

BOTH:

eyes all a - glow will find it hard to sleep to - night. They _ know that

San - ta's _ on his way; he's _ load-ed lots of toys _ and good - ies _ on his

sleigh, and _ ev-'ry moth-er's child _____ is _ gon-na spy to _ see if

rein - deer __ real-ly know how to fly _____ And so I'm of - fer - ing this

VOICE 2:   **VOICE 1:**

sim - ple phrase ____ to kids from one to ____ nine-ty - two, al -

BOTH:

though __ it's been said ____ man-y times, man-y ways, Mer - ry Christ - mas,

Mer - ry Christ - mas to you. _____

FELIZ NAVIDAD

Music and Lyrics by
JOSÉ FELICIANO

With a moderate Latin beat

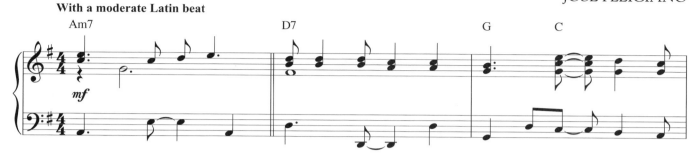

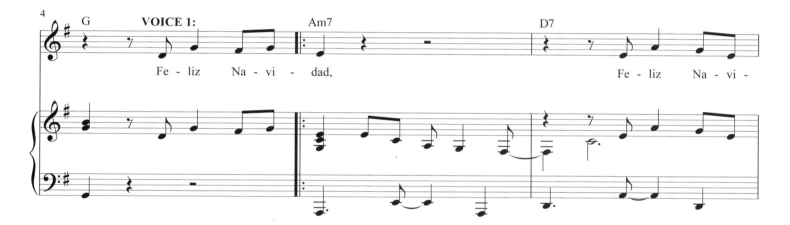

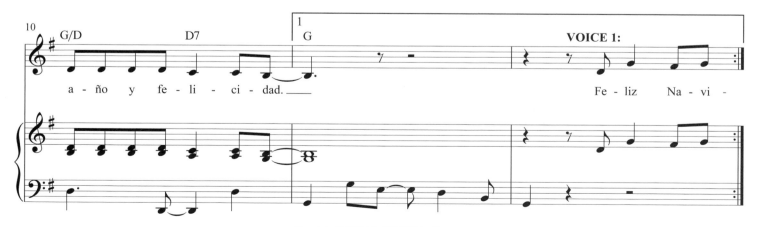

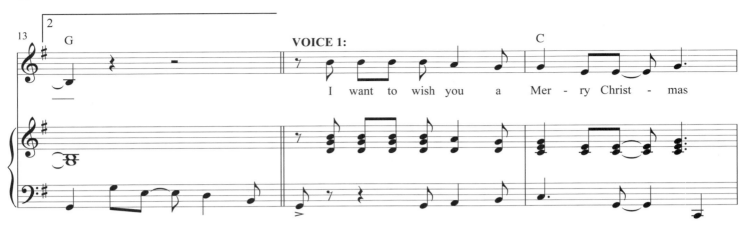

I want to wish you a Mer - ry Christ - mas

with lots of pres - ents to make you hap - py. I want to wish you a

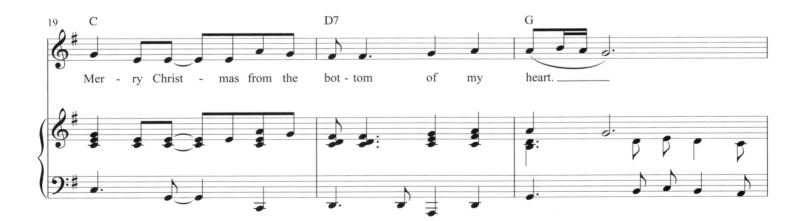

Mer - ry Christ - mas from the bot - tom of my heart.

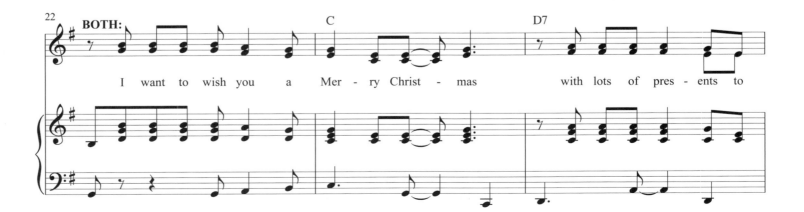

I want to wish you a Mer - ry Christ - mas with lots of pres - ents to

make you hap - py. I want to wish you a Mer - ry Christ - mas from the

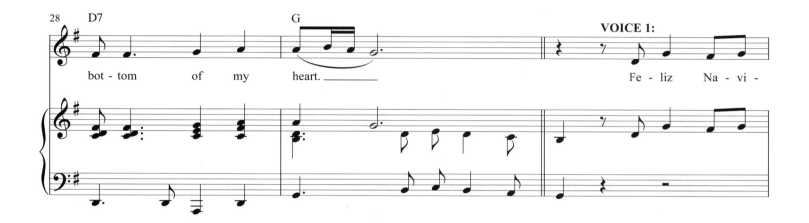

bot - tom of my heart. _____ **VOICE 1:** Fe - liz Na - vi -

dad, **VOICE 2:** Fe - liz Na - vi - dad, **BOTH:** Fe - liz Na - vi -

dad. Pros - per - o a - ño y fe - li - ci - dad. ___

CHRISTMAS TIME IS HERE

from A CHARLIE BROWN CHRISTMAS

Words by LEE MENDELSON
Music by VINCE GUARALDI

HAVE YOURSELF A MERRY LITTLE CHRISTMAS

from MEET ME IN ST. LOUIS

Words and Music by HUGH MARTIN
and RALPH BLANE

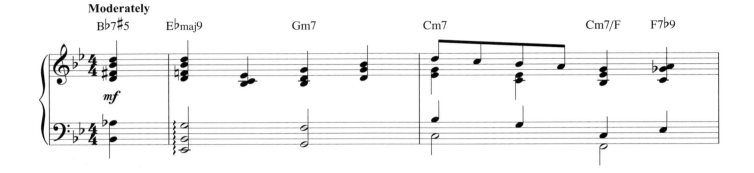

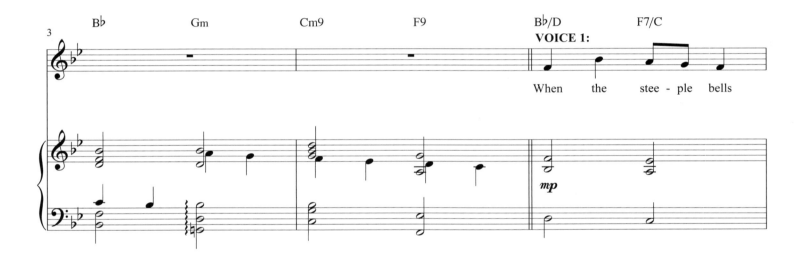

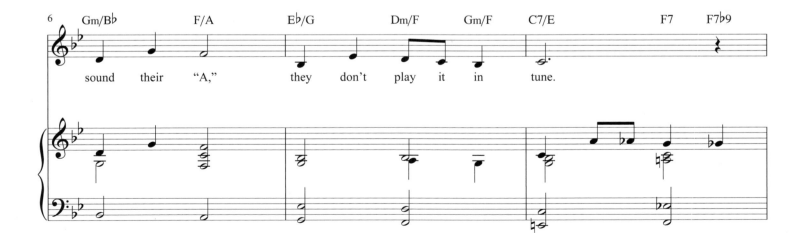

*An archaic English term for the highest celestial sphere.

20

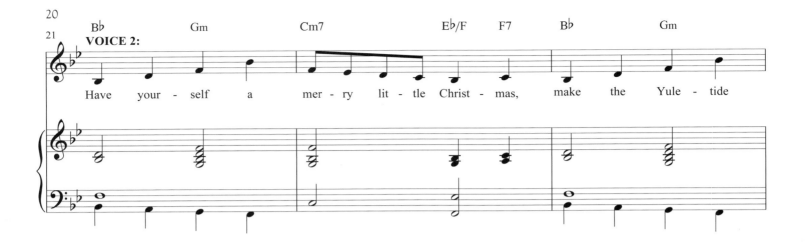

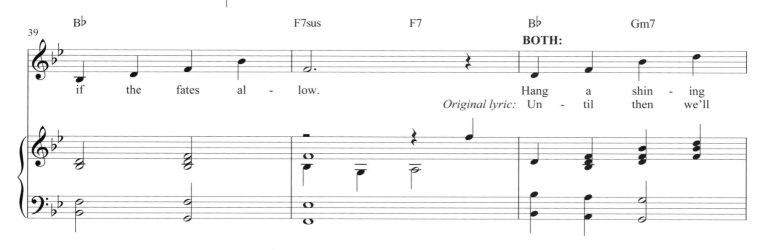

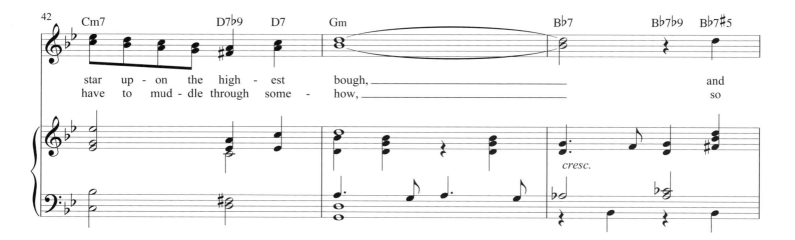

have your-self a mer-ry lit-tle Christ-mas now.

VOICE 1:

Here we are as in old-en days, hap-py

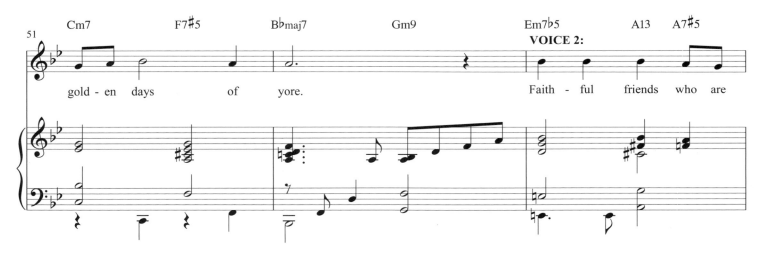

VOICE 2:

gold-en days of yore. Faith-ful friends who are

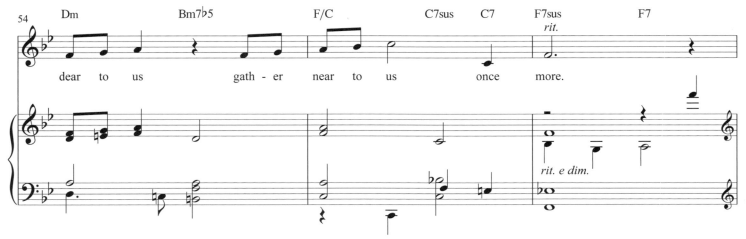

dear to us gath-er near to us once more.

Through the years we all will be to-geth - er, if the fates al -

BOTH:

low. Hang a shin - ing star up - on the high - est

Original lyric: Un - til then we'll have to mud - dle through some -

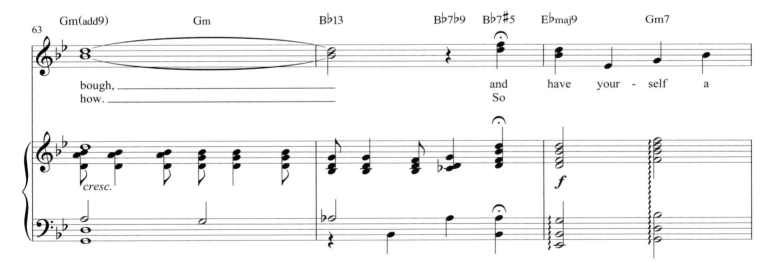

bough, _____
how. _____ and have your - self a
So

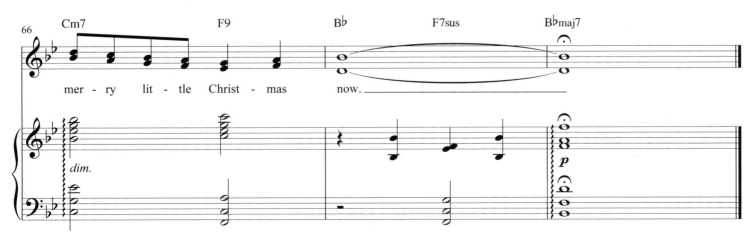

mer - ry lit - tle Christ - mas now. _____

A HOLLY JOLLY CHRISTMAS

Music and Lyrics by
JOHNNY MARKS

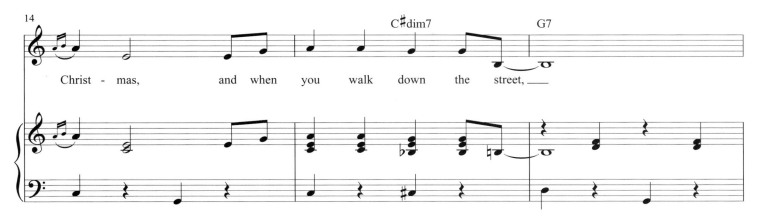

Christ - mas, and when you walk down the street, ____

say hel - lo to friends you know and ev - 'ry - one you

VOICE 1:

meet. Oh, ho, the mis - tle - toe hung where you can

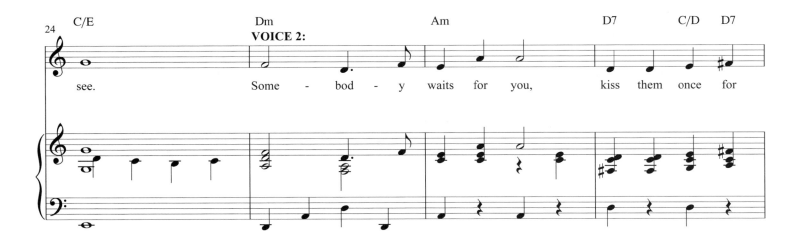

VOICE 2:

see. Some - bod - y waits for you, kiss them once for

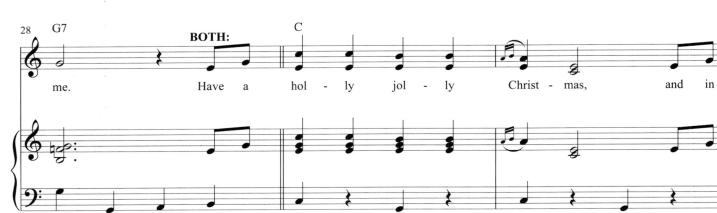

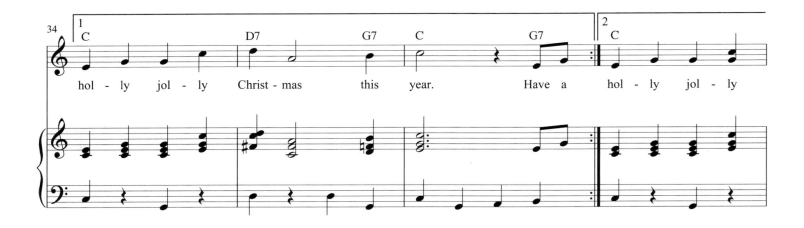

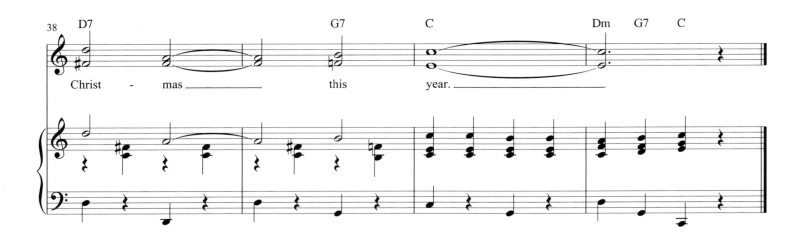

MARY, DID YOU KNOW?

Words and Music by MARK LOWRY
and BUDDY GREENE

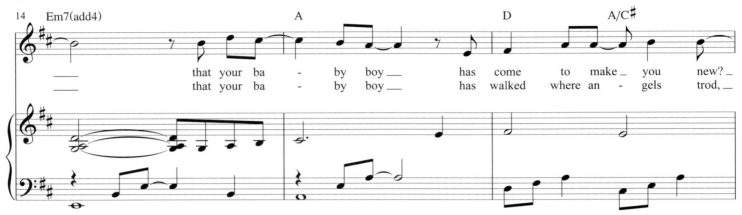

that your ba - by boy __ has come to make __ you new? __
that your ba - by boy __ has walked where an - gels trod, __

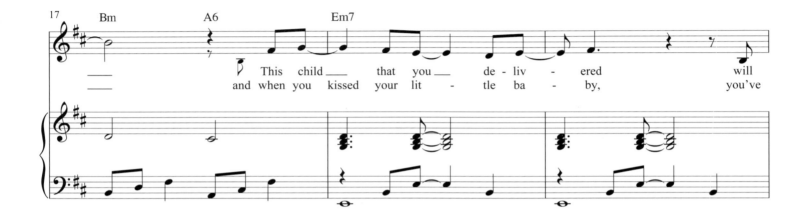

This child __ that you __ de - liv - ered will
and when you kissed your lit - tle ba - by, you've

soon de - liv - er you. _____ Mar - y, did you
kissed the face __ of God? __ Oh, Mar - y, did you

know? __

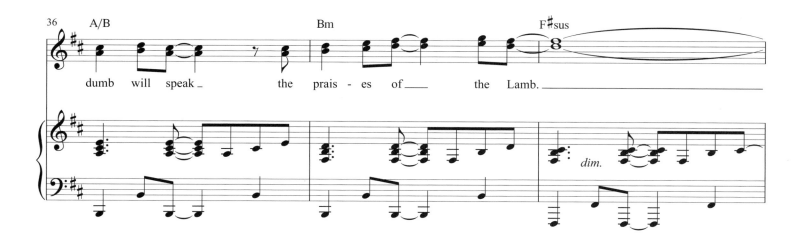

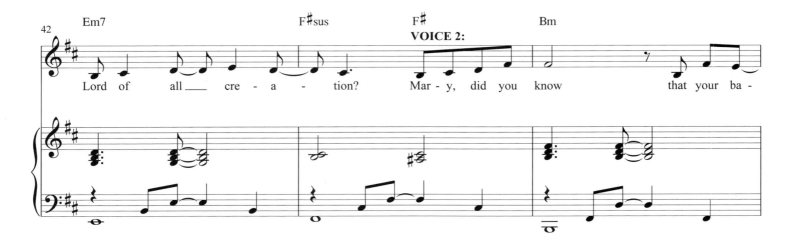

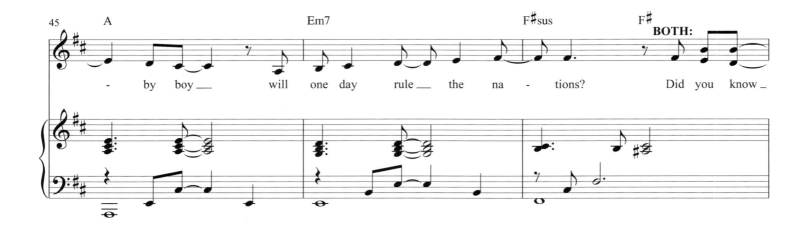

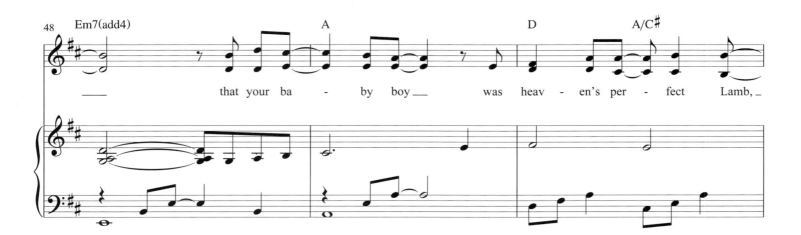

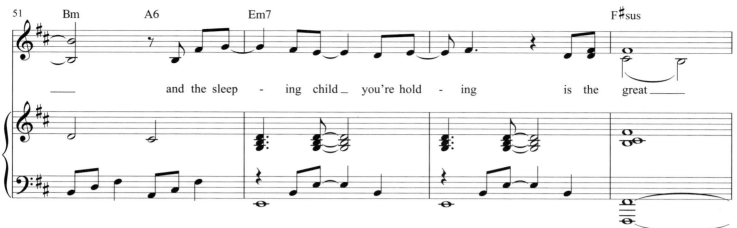

and the sleep - ing child___ you're hold - ing___ is the great___

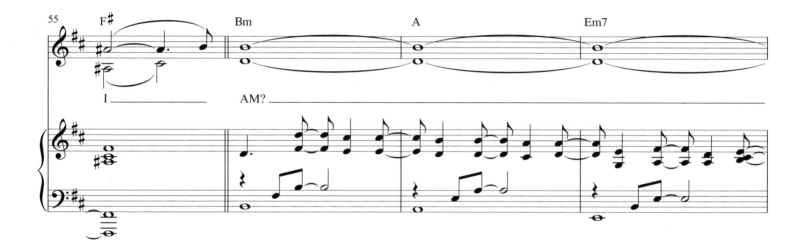

I ___ AM? ___

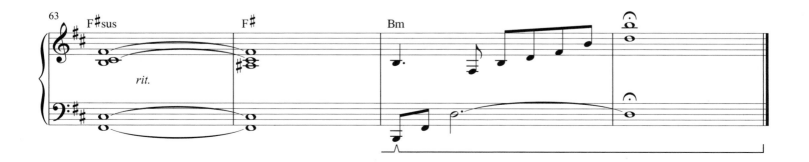

MERRY CHRISTMAS, DARLING

Words and Music by RICHARD CARPENTER
and FRANK POOLER

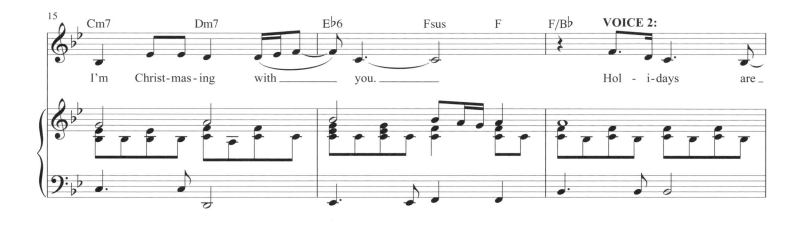

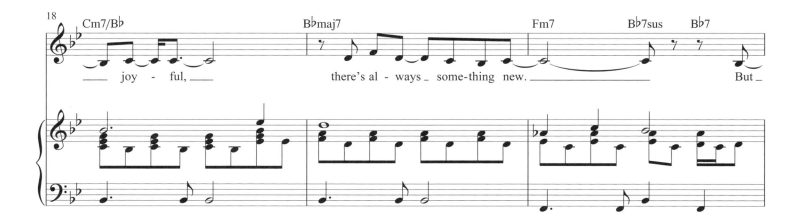

34

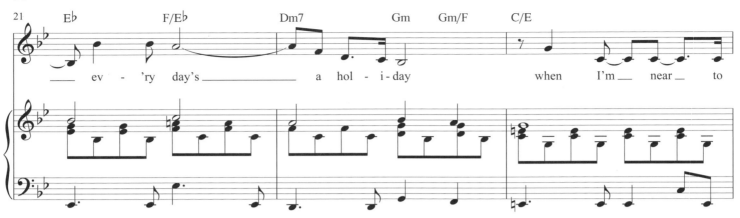

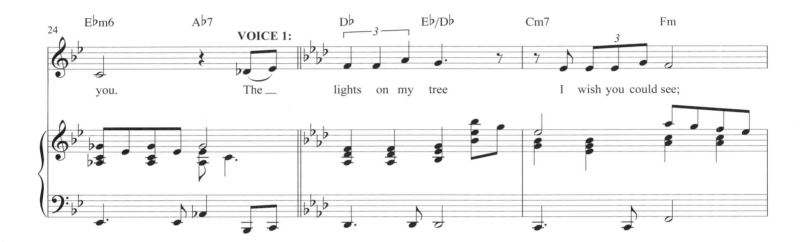

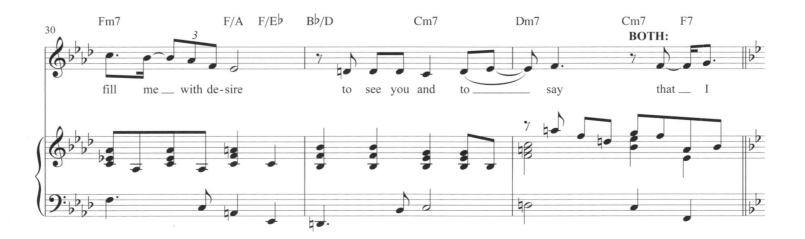

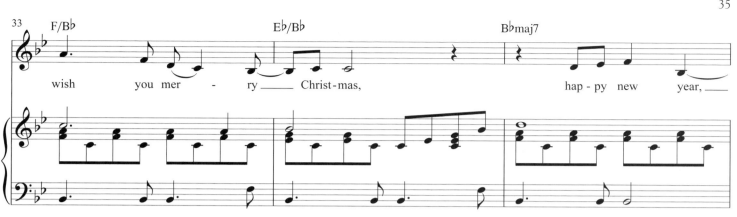

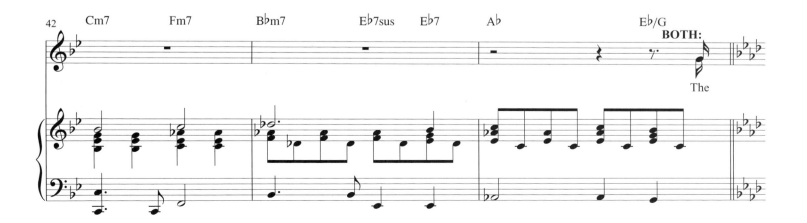

45

Fm   Fm(maj7)   Fm7   F/A   F/E♭   B♭/D   Cm7

logs   on   the   fire   fill   me __ with de-sire   to   see   you   and   to ____

Ooo _____   to   see   you   and   to ____

48

Dm7   Cm7   F7   F/B♭   E♭/B♭

__ say   that __ I   wish   you   mer -   ry ____ Christ-mas,

__ say   that __ I   wish   you   mer -   ry ____ Christ-mas,

51

B♭maj7   Fm9   B♭7sus   F♭13#11   E♭   F/E♭

hap - py   new   year, ____ too. ____ I've ____ just __ one   wish   on   this

hap - py   new   year, ____ too. ____ I've ____ just __ one   wish   on   this

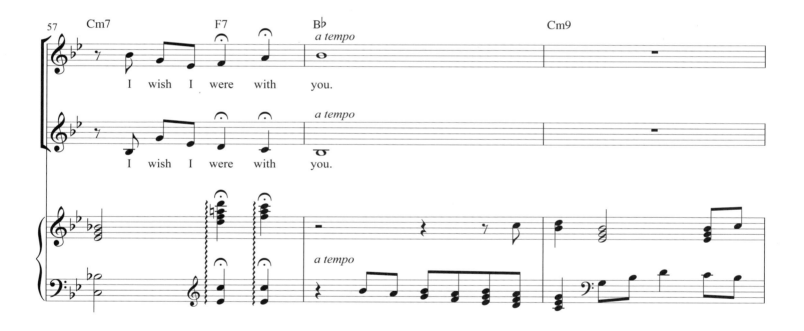

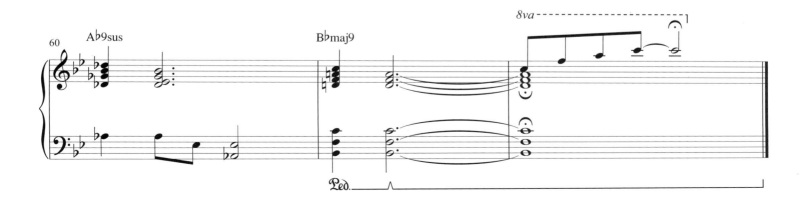

THE MOST WONDERFUL TIME OF THE YEAR

Words and Music by EDDIE POLA
and GEORGE WYLE

There'll be par-ties for host-ing, marsh-mal-lows for toast-ing and

car-ol-ing out in the snow. There'll be scar-y ghost

sto-ries and tales of the glo-ries of Christ-mas-es long, long a-

go. _____ It's the most won-der-ful time _____

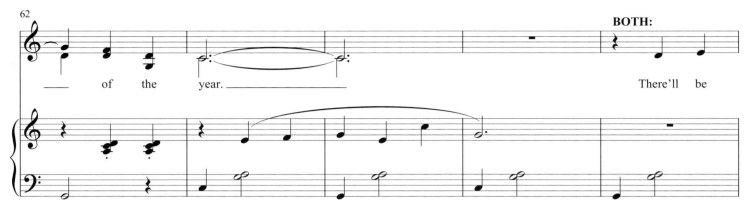

BOTH:

of the year. _____ There'll be

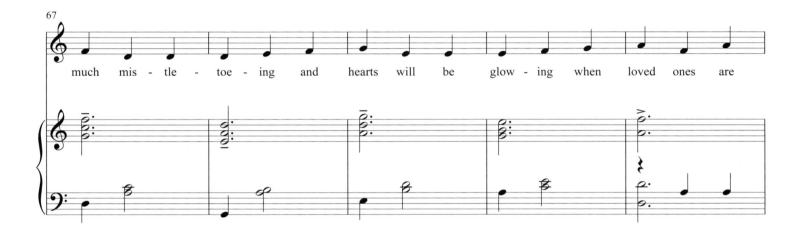

much mis - tle - toe - ing and hearts will be glow - ing when loved ones are

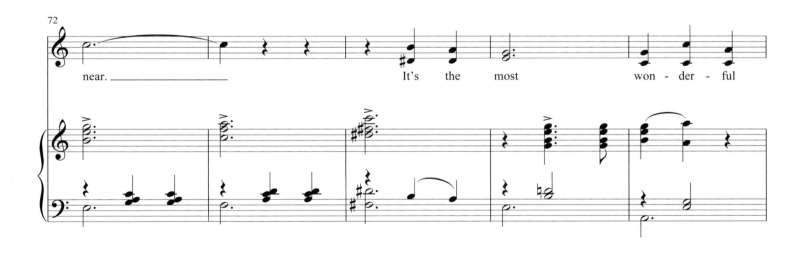

near. _____ It's the most won - der - ful

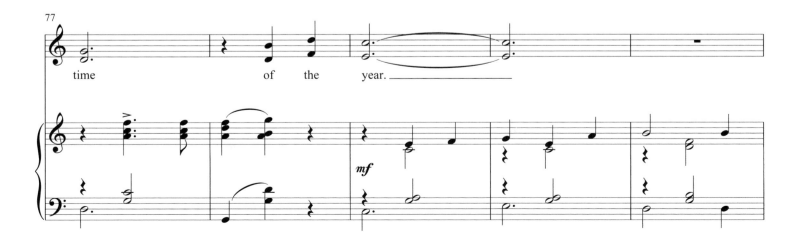

time of the year. _____

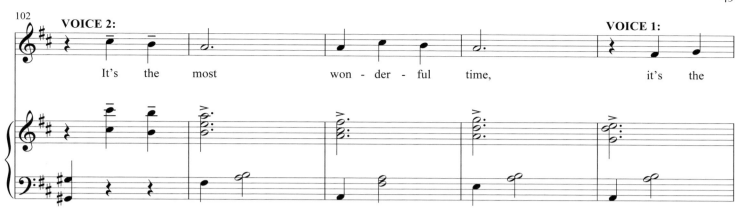

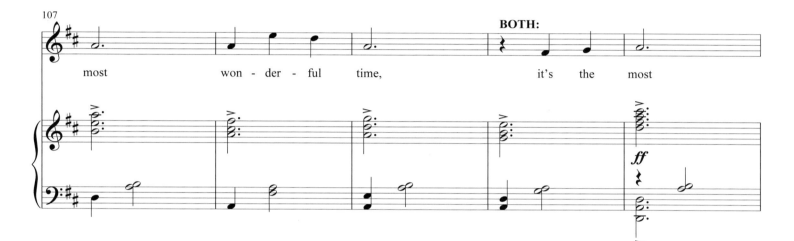

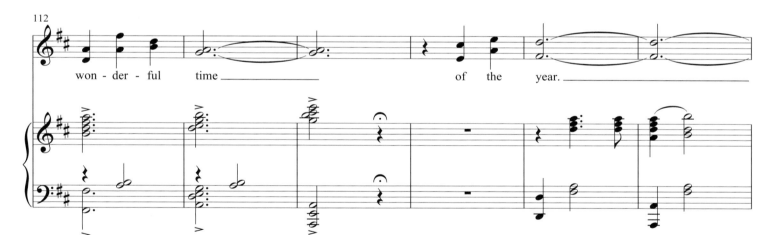

O HOLY NIGHT
(Cantique de Noël)

French Words by PLACIDE CAPPEAU
English Words by JOHN S. DWIGHT
Music by ADOLPHE ADAM

Andante maestoso

O ho - ly night! ___ the stars are bright - ly

O ho - ly night! ___ the stars are bright - ly

shin - ing, It is the night of the dear Sav - iour's birth.

shin - ing, It is the night of the dear Sav - iour's birth.

Long lay the world ___ in sin and er - ror pin - ing Till He ap-

Long lay the world ___ in sin and er - ror pin - ing Till He ap-

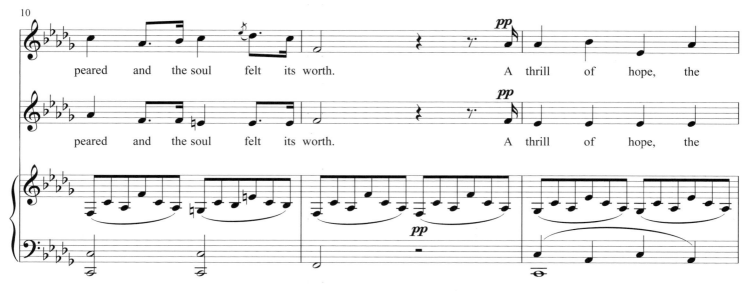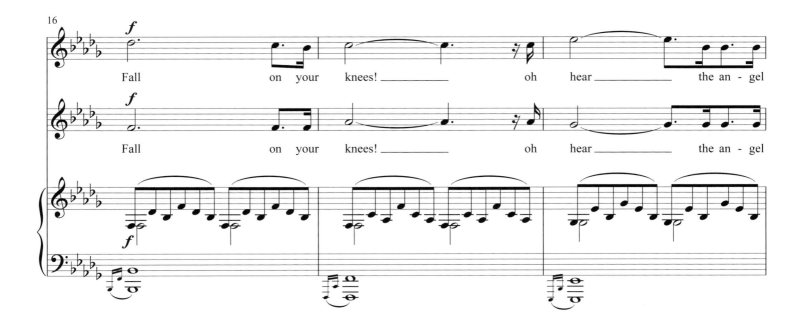

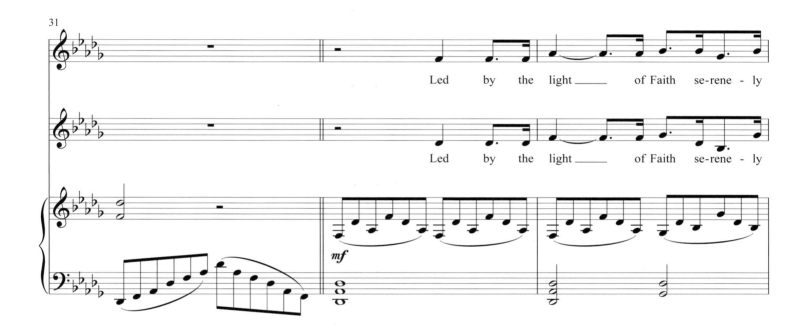

Led by the light ____ of Faith se-rene - ly

Led by the light ____ of Faith se-rene - ly

beam - ing, With glow - ing hearts by His cra - dle we stand.

beam - ing, With glow - ing hearts by His cra - dle we stand.

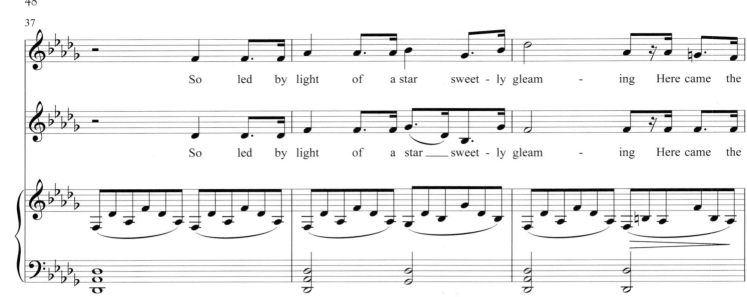

So led by light of a star sweet-ly gleam - ing Here came the

So led by light of a star sweet-ly gleam - ing Here came the

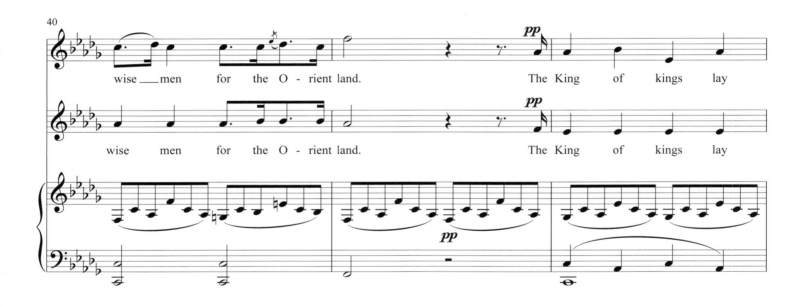

wise men for the O - rient land. The King of kings lay

wise men for the O - rient land. The King of kings lay

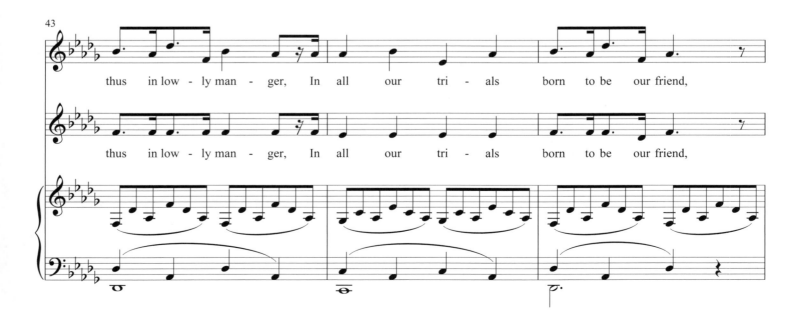

thus in low - ly man - ger, In all our tri - als born to be our friend,

thus in low - ly man - ger, In all our tri - als born to be our friend,

He knows our need, _____ He guard - eth us from

He knows our need, _____ He guard - eth us from

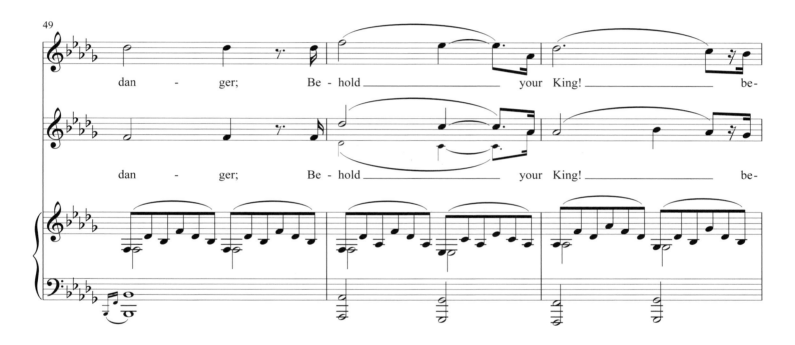

dan - ger; Be - hold _____ your King! _____ be-

dan - ger; Be - hold _____ your King! _____ be-

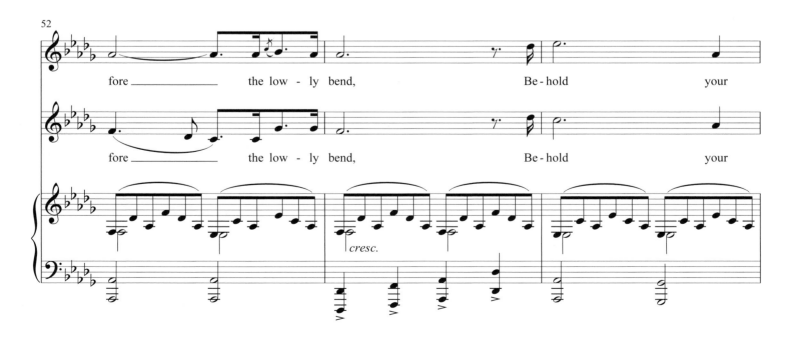

fore _____ the low - ly bend, Be - hold your

fore _____ the low - ly bend, Be - hold your

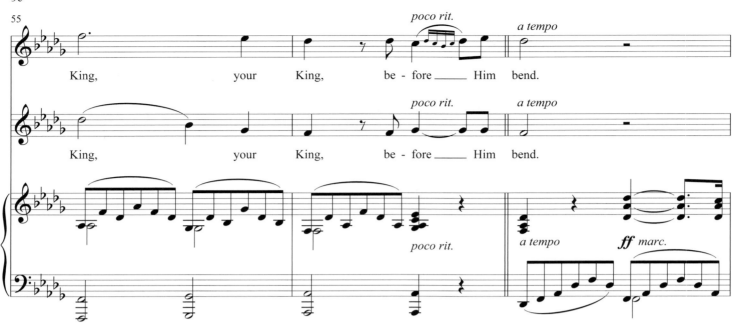

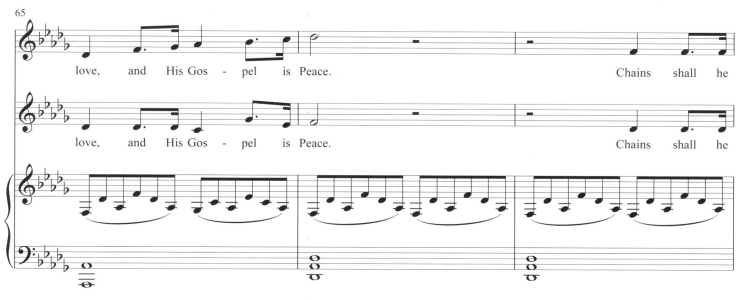

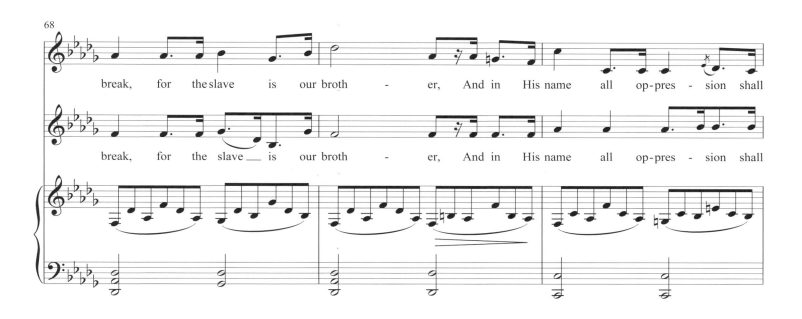

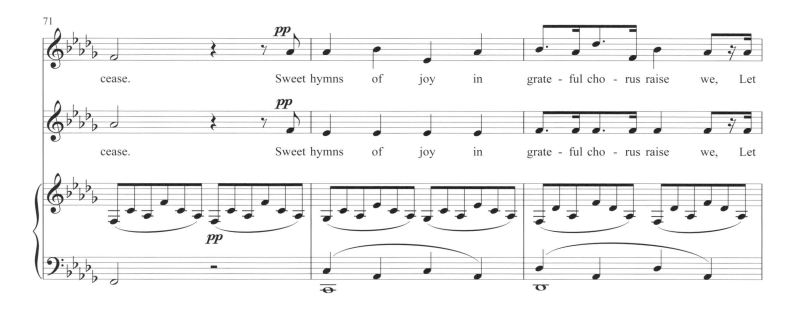

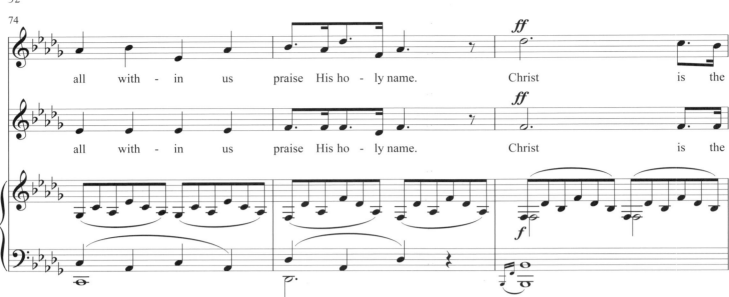

all with - in us praise His ho - ly name. Christ is the

all with - in us praise His ho - ly name. Christ is the

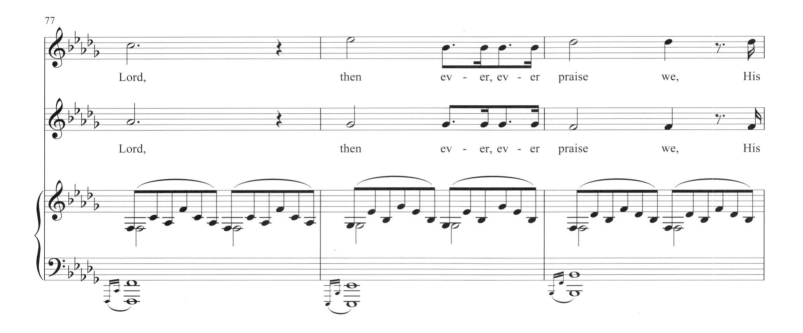

Lord, then ev - er, ev - er praise we, His

Lord, then ev - er, ev - er praise we, His

pow'r _____ and glo - ry __ ev - er-more pro-

pow'r _____ and glo - ry __ ev - er-more pro-

claim,   His pow'r _____ and glo - ry

claim,   His pow'r _____ and glo - ry

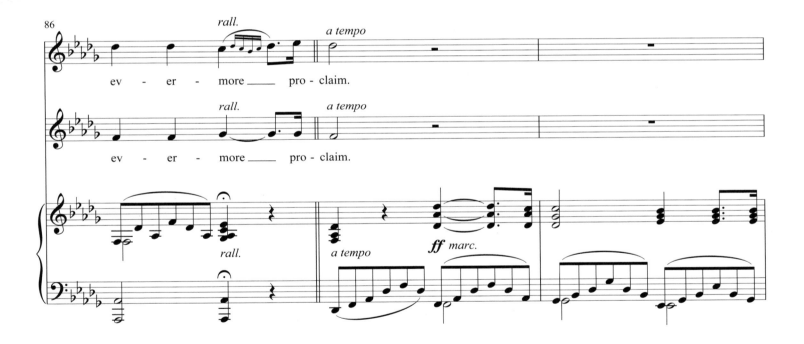

ev - er - more _____ pro - claim.

ev - er - more _____ pro - claim.

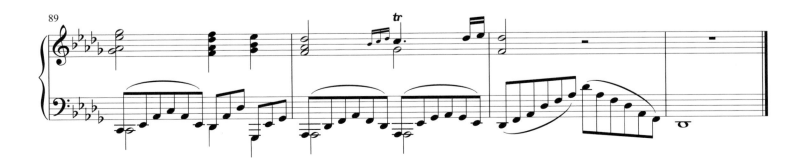

SILVER BELLS
from the Paramount Picture THE LEMON DROP KID

Words and Music by JAY LIVINGSTON
and RAY EVANS

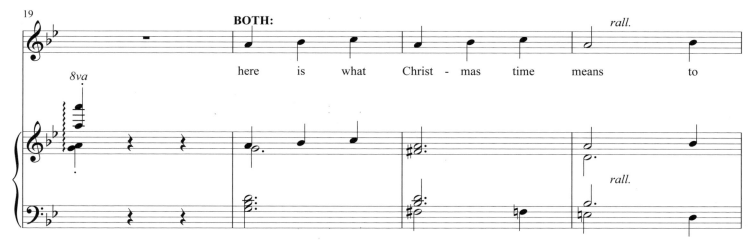

here is what Christ - mas time means to

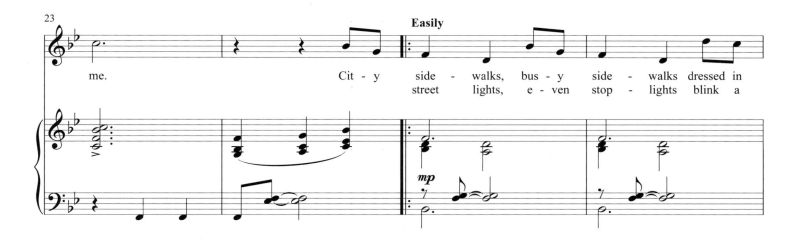

me.   Cit - y side - walks, bus - y side - walks dressed in
       street lights, e - ven stop - lights blink a

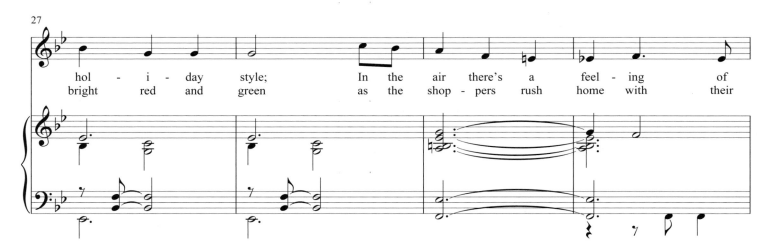

hol - i - day style;   In the air there's a feel - ing of
bright red and green   as the shop - pers rush home with their

VOICE 1:

Christ - mas. _____ Chil - dren laugh - ing, peo - ple pass - ing, meet - ing
treas - ures. _____ Hear the snow crunch, see the kids bunch, this is

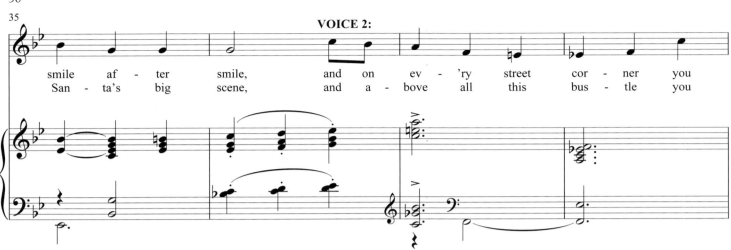

VOICE 2:

smile af - ter smile, and on ev - 'ry street cor - ner you
San - ta's big scene, and a - bove all this bus - tle you

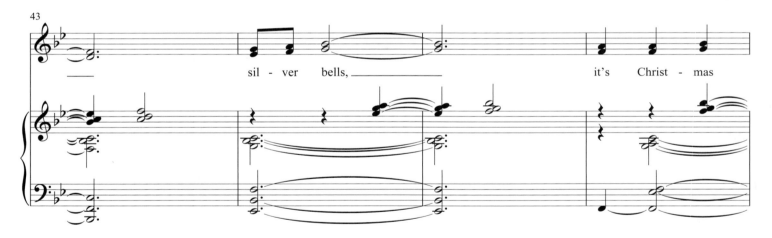

BOTH:

hear: _____
hear: _____

Sil - ver bells, _____

____ sil - ver bells, _____ it's Christ - mas

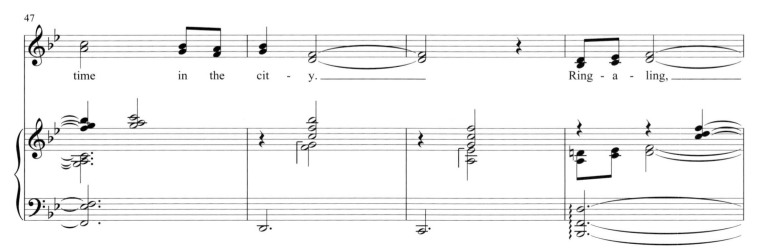

time in the cit - y. _____ Ring - a - ling, _____

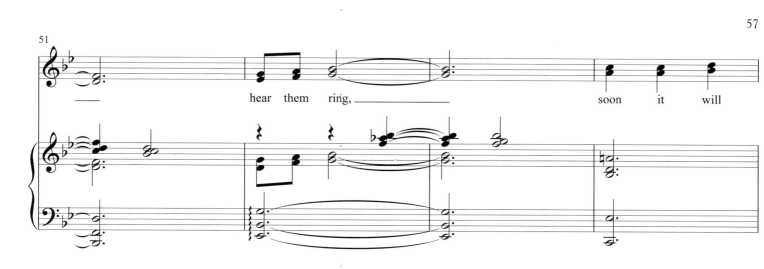

hear them ring, _____ soon it will

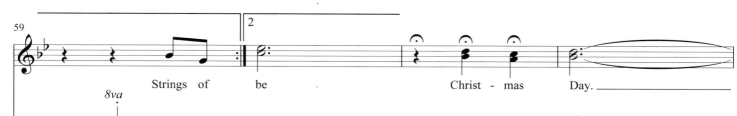

be Christ - mas Day. _____

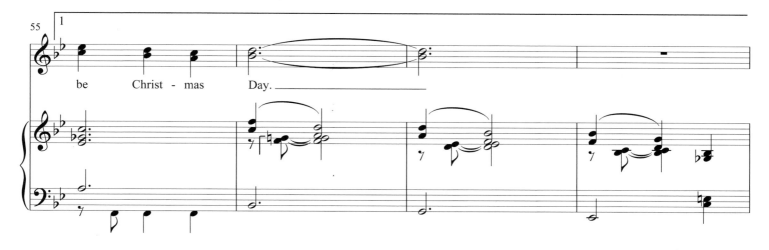

Strings of be Christ - mas Day. _____

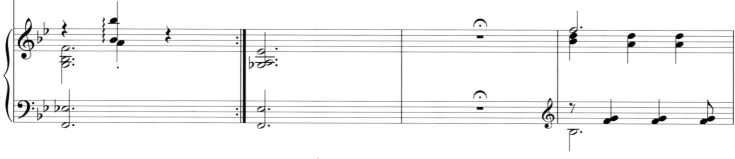

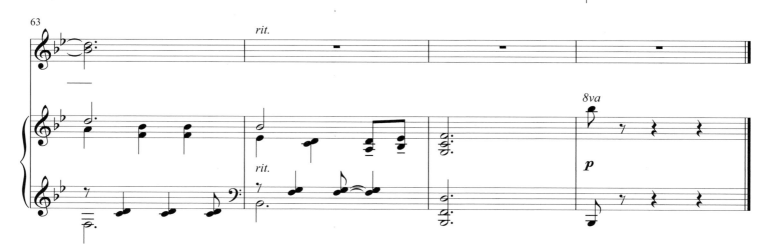

rit.

WALKING IN THE AIR
from THE SNOWMAN

Words and Music by
HOWARD BLAKE

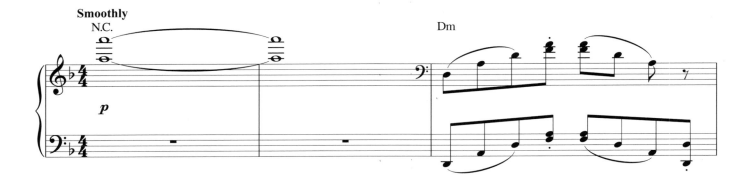

We're walk-ing in the air, _____ we're

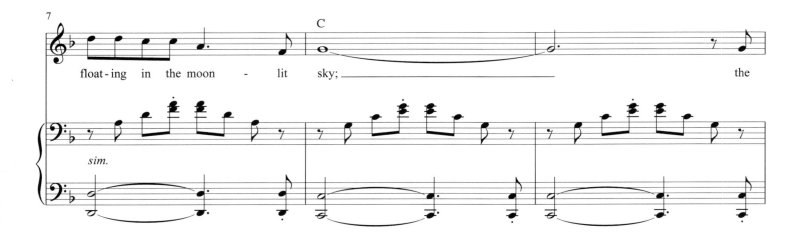

float-ing in the moon - lit sky; _____ the

find-ing I can fly so high a-bove with you._____

blue, so high a-bove with you, rid-ing in the mid - night

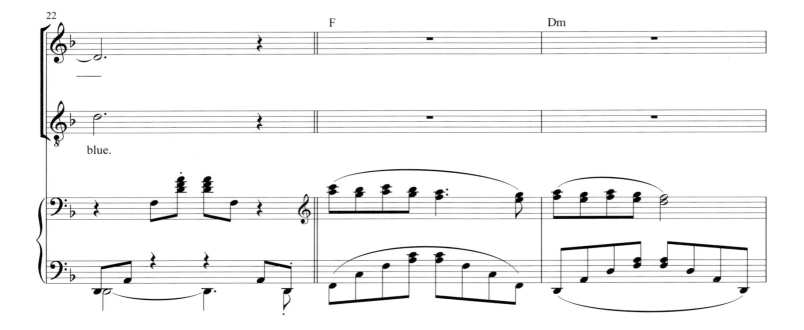

blue.

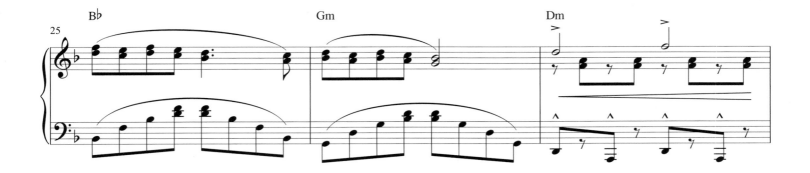

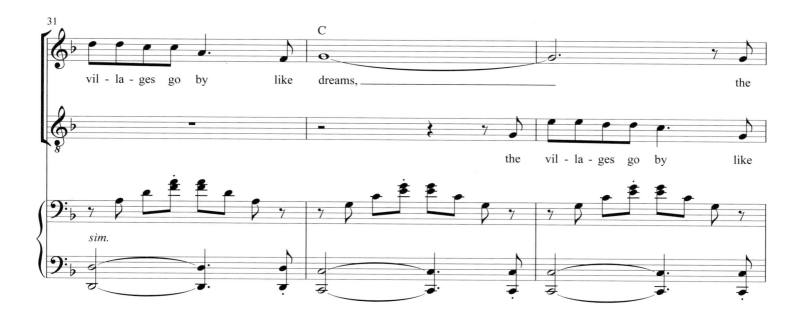

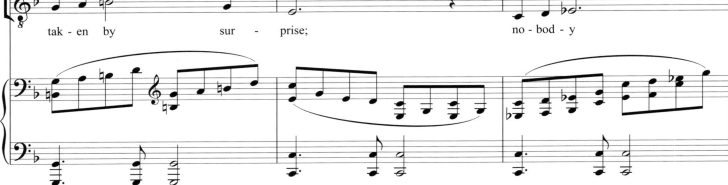

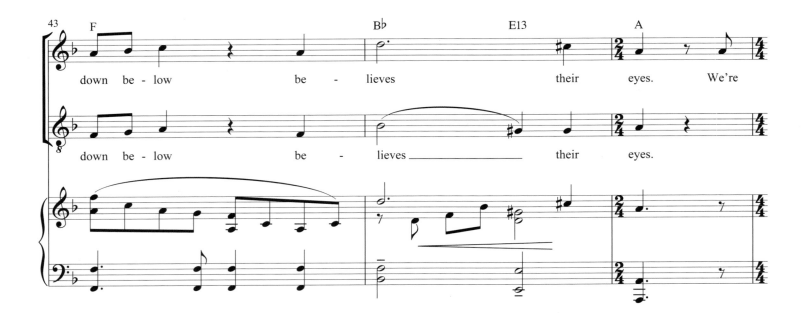

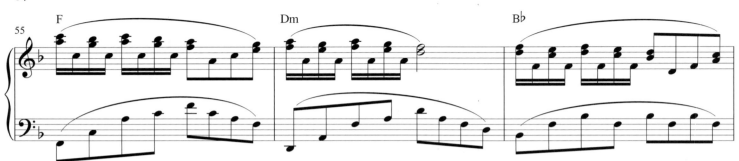

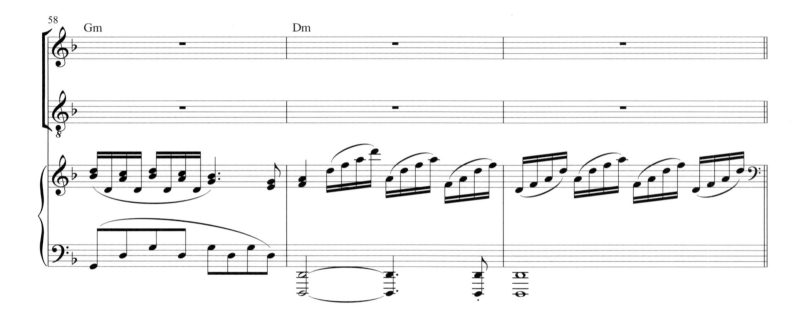

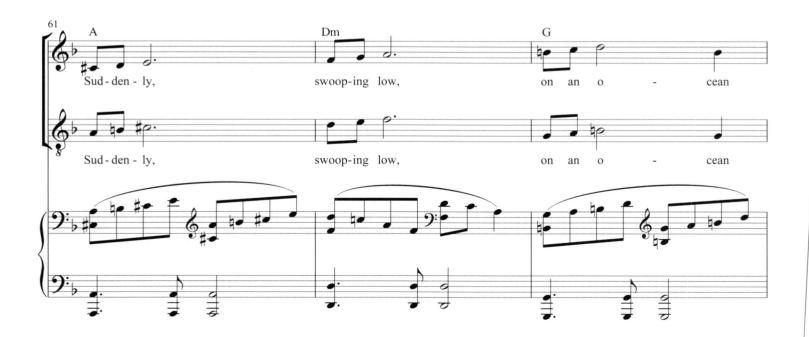

Sud - den - ly,　　　　　swoop-ing low,　　　　　on an o - cean

Sud - den - ly,　　　　　swoop-ing low,　　　　　on an o - cean

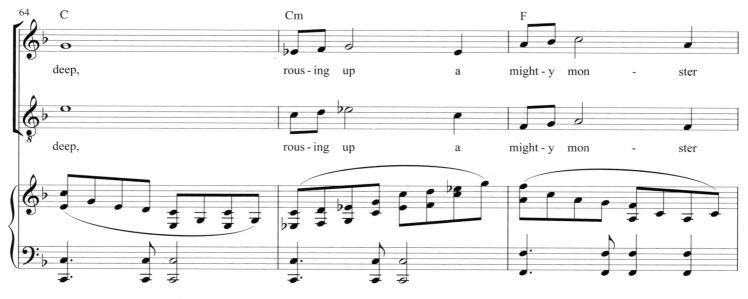

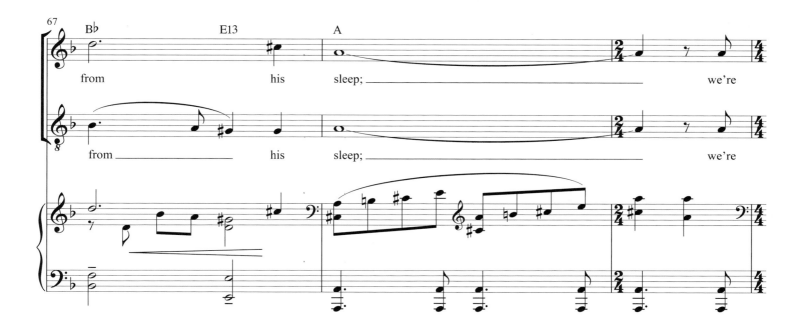

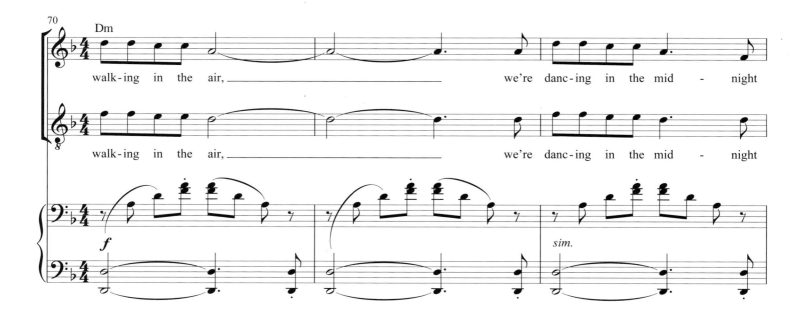

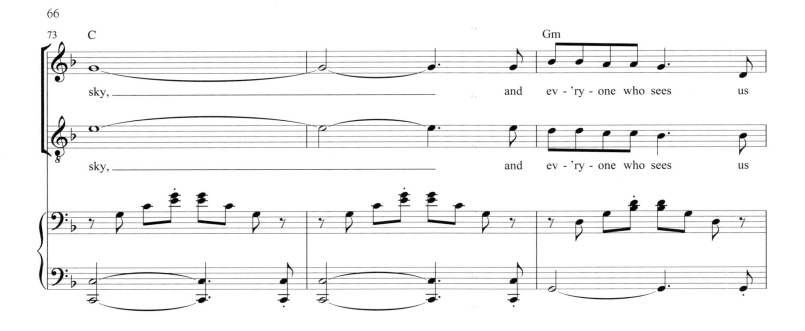

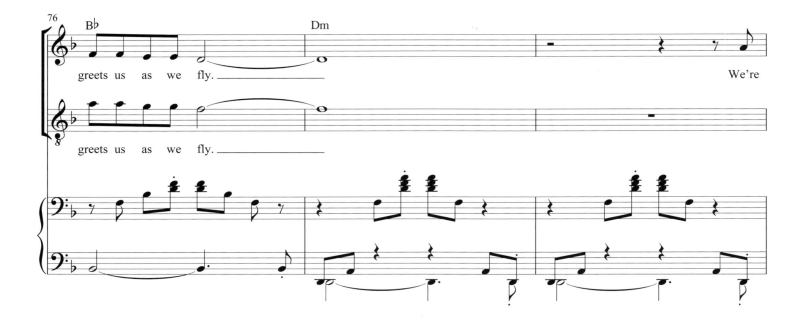

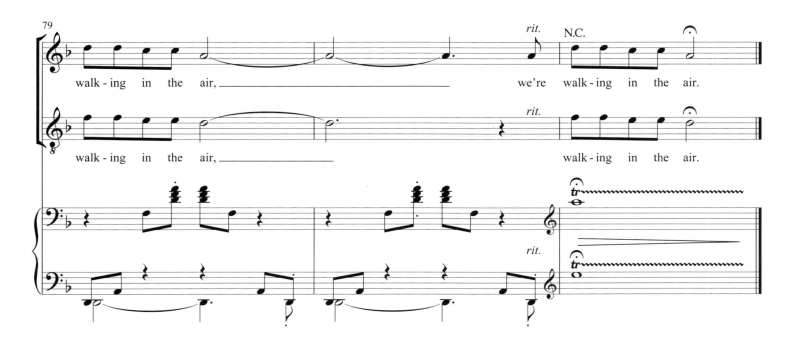

SLEIGH RIDE

Music by LEROY ANDERSON
Words by MITCHELL PARISH

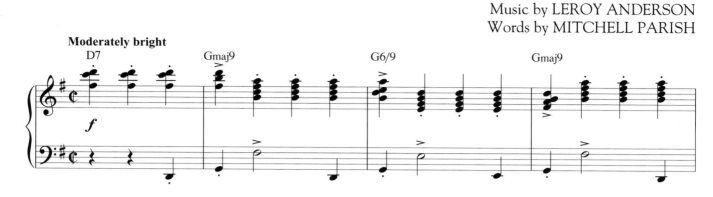

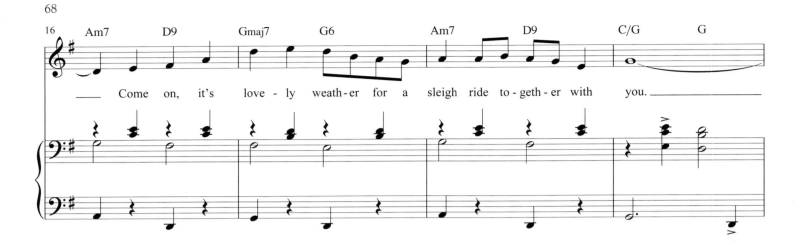

Come on, it's love-ly weath-er for a sleigh ride to-geth-er with you. ___

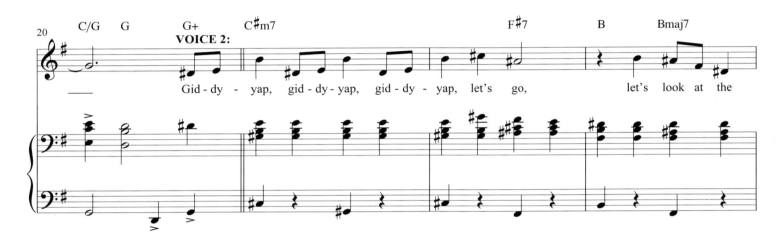

VOICE 2:

Gid - dy - yap, gid-dy-yap, gid-dy-yap, let's go, let's look at the

show. We're rid-ing in a won-der-land of snow. ___

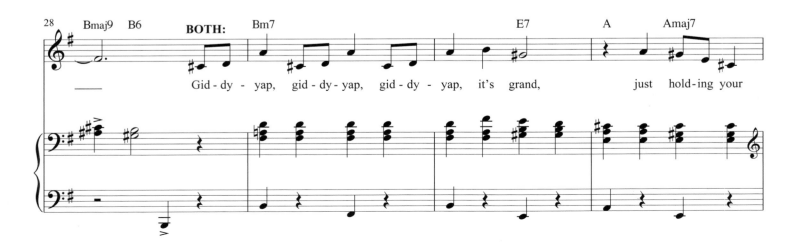

BOTH:

Gid-dy-yap, gid-dy-yap, gid-dy-yap, it's grand, just hold-ing your

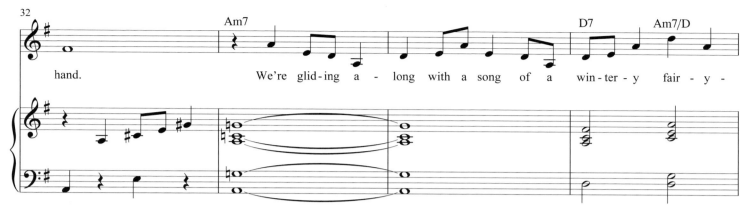

hand. We're glid-ing a - long with a song of a win-ter-y fair-y-

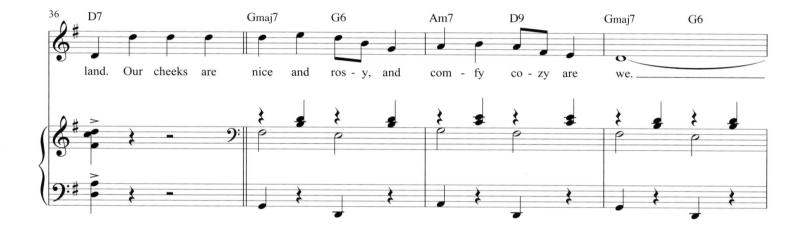

land. Our cheeks are nice and ros-y, and com-fy co-zy are we. _____

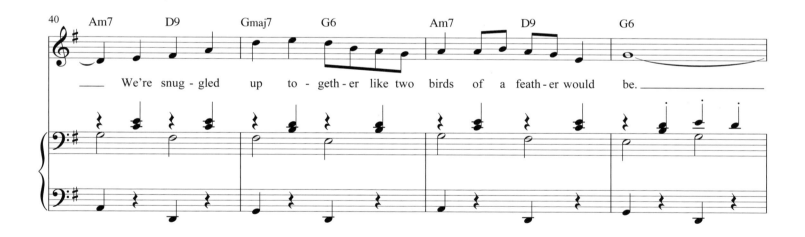

_____ We're snug-gled up to-geth-er like two birds of a feath-er would be. _____

VOICE 1:

_____ Let's take that road be-fore us and sing a cho-rus or two. _____

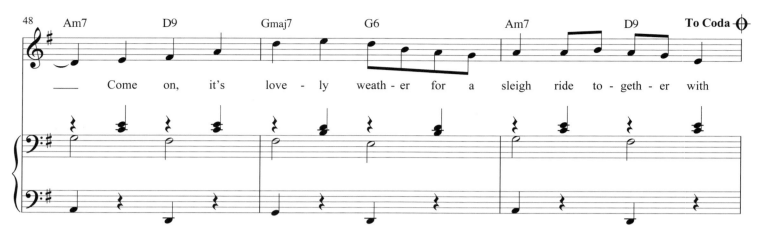

Come on, it's love-ly weath-er for a sleigh ride to-geth-er with

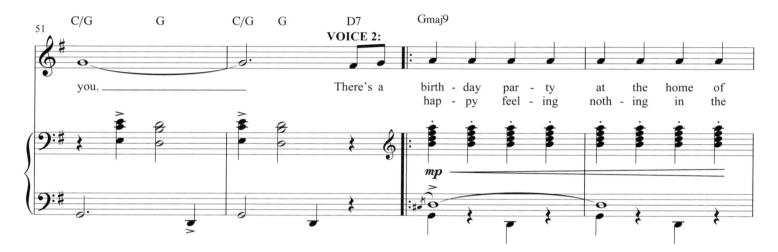

you. _____ **VOICE 2:** There's a birth-day par-ty at the home of
hap-py feel-ing noth-ing in the

Farm - er Gray. It-'ll be the per-fect end-ing of a
world can buy, when they pass a-round the cof-fee and the

per - fect day. **BOTH:** We'll be sing-ing the songs we love to sing with-
pump - kin pie. It-'ll near-ly be like a pic-ture print by

71

WHITE CHRISTMAS

from the Motion Picture Irving Berlin's HOLIDAY INN

Words and Music by
IRVING BERLIN

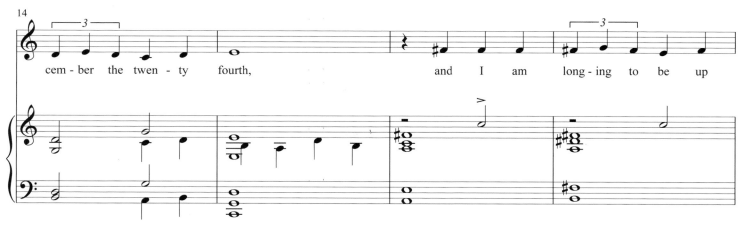

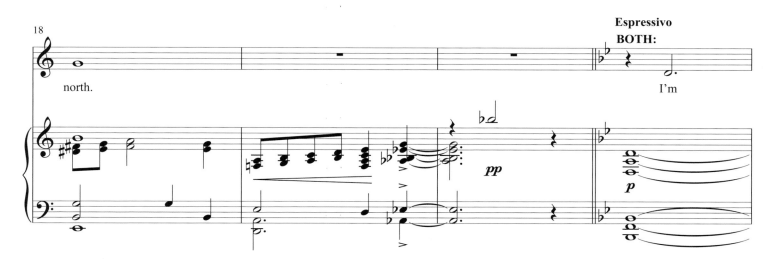

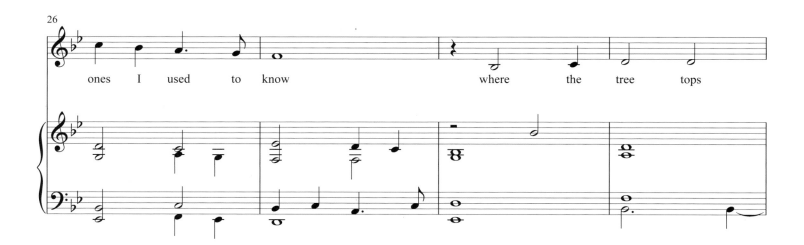

glis - ten and chil - dren lis - ten to hear

sleigh bells in the snow.

VOICE 1:

I'm

dream - ing of a white Christ - mas. With ev - 'ry

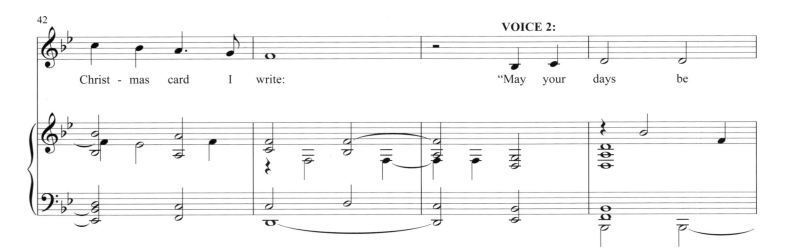

Christ - mas card I write:

VOICE 2:

"May your days be

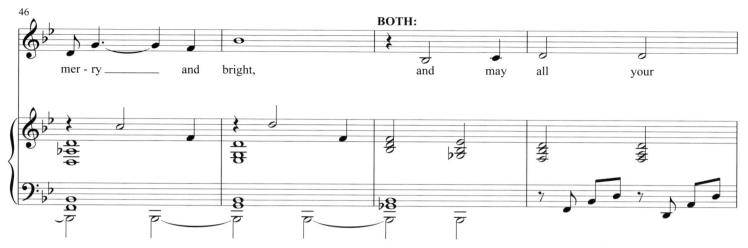

mer - ry _____ and bright, and may all your

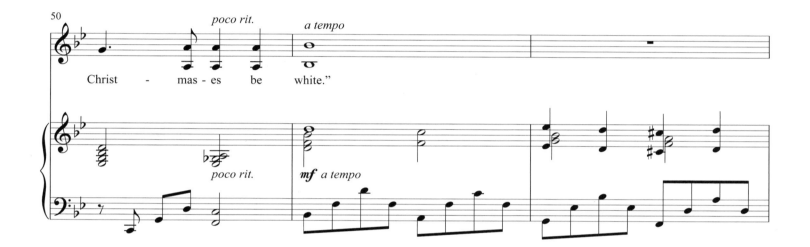

poco rit. *a tempo*

Christ - mas - es be white."

poco rit. **mf** *a tempo*

poco rit. *a tempo*

Where the tree tops

poco rit. *a tempo*

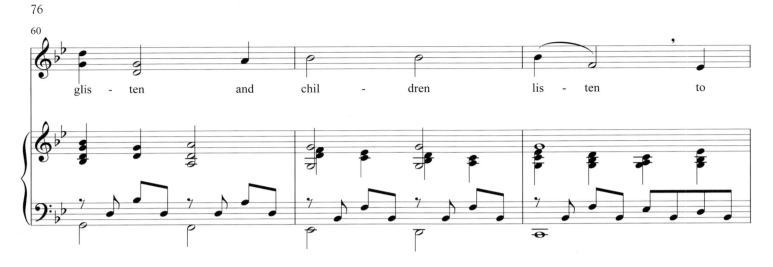

glis - ten and chil - dren lis - ten to

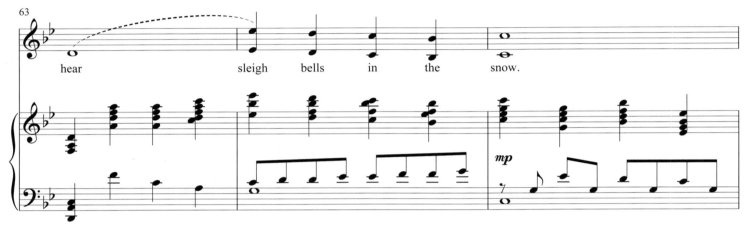

hear sleigh bells in the snow.

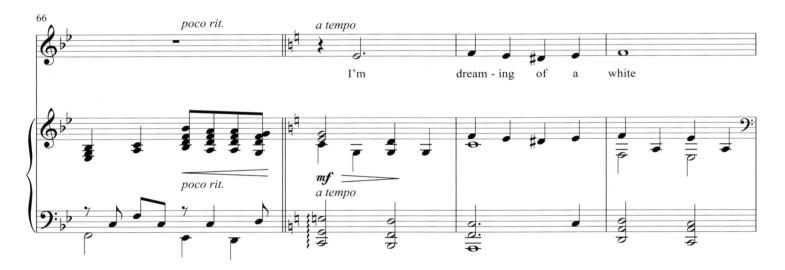

I'm dream - ing of a white

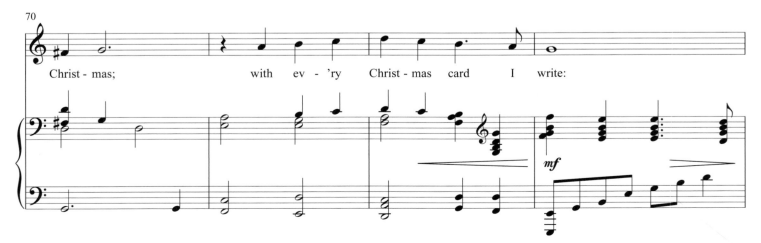

Christ - mas; with ev - 'ry Christ - mas card I write:

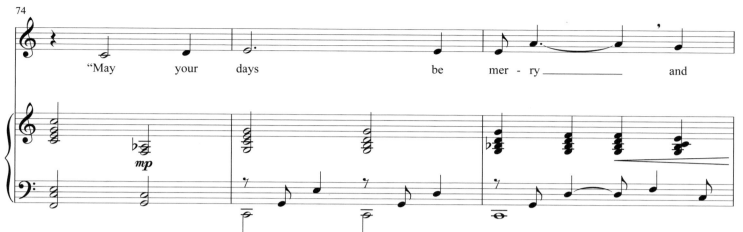

"May your days be mer - ry _____ and

bright _____ and may

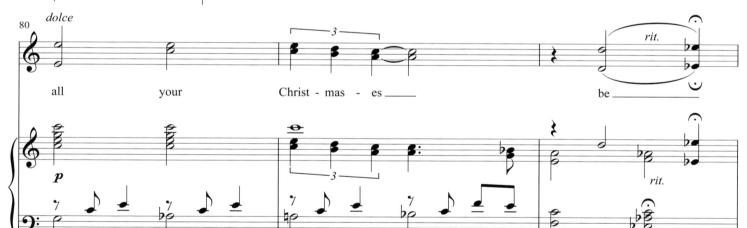

all your Christ - mas - es _____ be _____

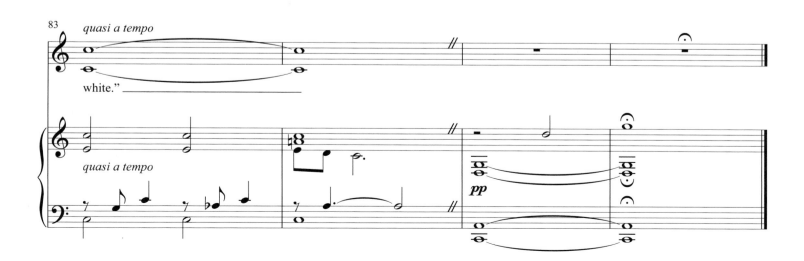

white." _____

WINTER WONDERLAND

Words by DICK SMITH
Music by FELIX BERNARD

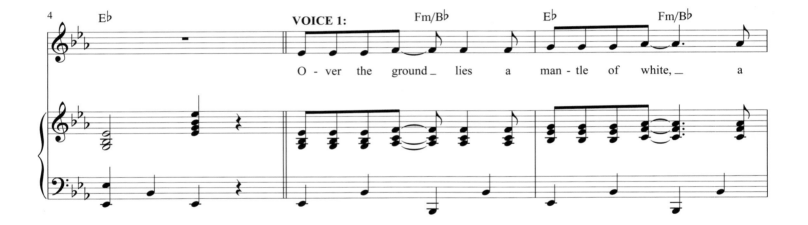

O - ver the ground lies a man - tle of white, a

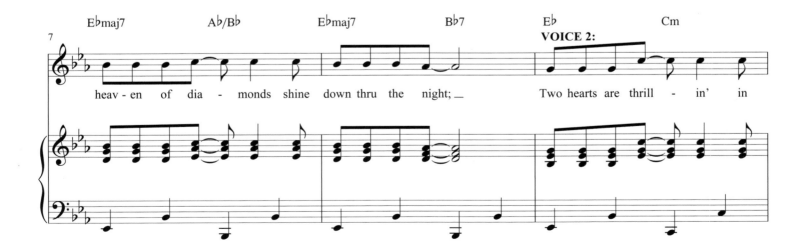

heav - en of dia - monds shine down thru the night; Two hearts are thrill - in' in

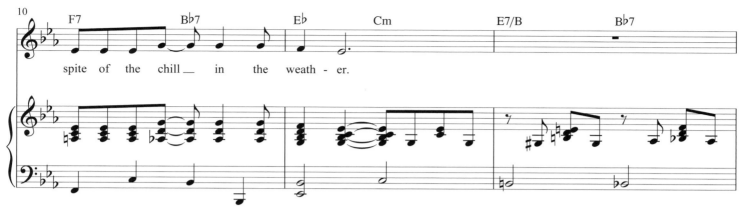

spite of the chill __ in the weath - er.

VOICE 1:

Love knows no sea - son; love knows no clime; __ ro - mance can blos - som

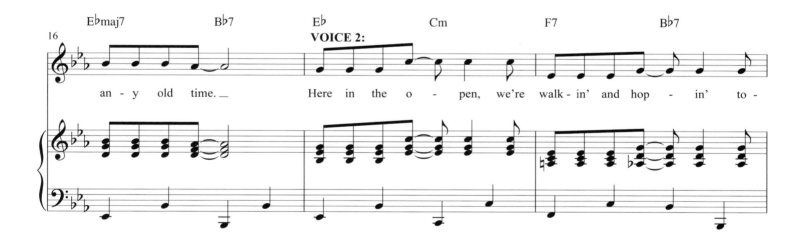

an - y old time. __ Here in the o - pen, we're walk - in' and hop - in' to -

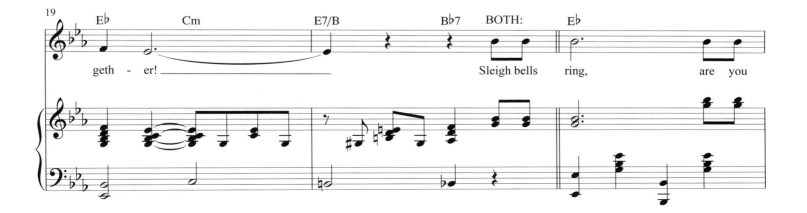

geth - er! _____ Sleigh bells ring, are you

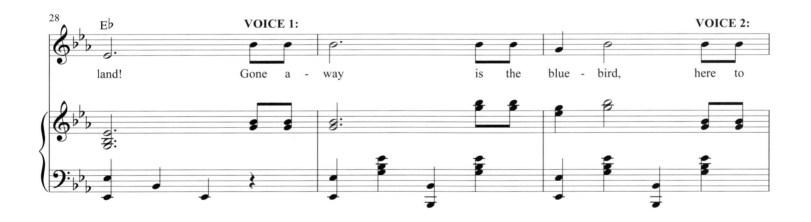

we go a - long, _____ walk - in' in a win - ter won - der - land! _____

VOICE 1:

In the mead - ow we can build a snow - man,
{ then pre - tend that he is Par - son
{ and pre - tend that he's a cir - cus

VOICE 2:

Brown; _____ He'll say, "Are you mar - ried?" We'll say, "No, man! But
clown; _____ We'll have lots of fun with Mis - ter Snow - man, un -

VOICE 1:

you can do the job when you're in town!" Lat - er on, we'll con -
til the oth - er kid - dies knock 'im down! When it snows, ain't it

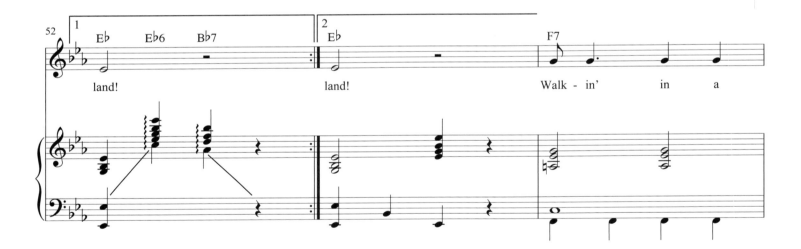

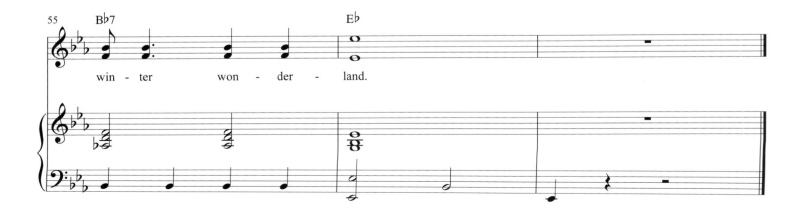